Off The Cuff

Off The Cuff

C A & I E Parr

Mudderbee Publications

Copyright © C A & I E Parr 2005
First published in 2005 by Mudderbee Publications
33 Tylney Avenue, Rochford, Essex SS4 1QP
Illustrations © Dandi Palmer 2005

Distributed by Gazelle Book Services Limited
Hightown, White Cross Mills, South Rd, Lancaster, England LA1 4XS

British Library Cataloguing in Publication Data
A catalogue record for this book is available from the British Library

ISBN 0-9549696-0-X

Typeset by Amolibros, Milverton, Somerset
This book production has been managed by Amolibros
Printed and bound by Advance Book Printing, Oxford, UK

'Off the Cuff' - Instructions

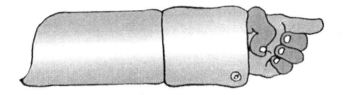

The game can be played by two or more people at any time and in any place - e.g. at a party, in the classroom, in the house or when travelling.

'Off the Cuff' is a brief story with words omitted. It is the job of the 'STORYTELLERS' to fill in the blank words as asked by the 'NARRATOR'.

The 'NARRATOR' is the only person to see the story before it is completed. He or she will ask his or her friends to fill in the blanks as indicated in the text. The 'NARRATOR' will then read the story out loud with the completed blanks. The resulting story will be stupid, ridiculous and usually hilarious.

Photocopy the pages or use a pencil and eraser in order to play the game again and again.

THE RULES OF GRAMMAR

(FOR THOSE OF US WHO HAVE FORGOTTEN)

A <u>NOUN</u> is an object or thing

Examples: -

sausage	bus	teapot
toilet	dog	building
chair	log	scissors
salt pot	slug	cigarette
aeroplane	jam	basket
flagpole	tree	signpost
bridge	ball	ashtray
classroom	gate	cupboard
candle	bell	saucer
whistle	flag	shampoo

A <u>VERB</u> expresses action

Examples: -

dance	walk	kiss
laugh	sit	cuddle
fetch	run	spank
whistle	jump	play
write	cry	shake
shout	put	tremble
whisper	sing	smoke
tickle	read	stand
strangle	love	work
wander	hate	hide

An <u>ADJECTIVE</u> is a 'describing' word

An <u>ADVERB</u> modifies the sentence and ends in 'ly'

Examples: -

Examples: -

handsome	fat	clever
spotty	slim	smelly
cool	wise	awesome
fantastic	ugly	stupid
beautiful	flat	great
magnificent	tiny	awful
cocky	cool	tubby
greasy	huge	hairy
wonderful	old	batty
ordinary	mad	droopy

unfortunately	sadly
apparently	happily
beautifully	stupidly
fantastically	greatly
carefully	awfully
magnificently	boldly
cockily	coolly
disgustedly	loudly
wonderfully	luckily
modestly	crazily

An <u>EXCLAMATION</u> is comment made when shocked or surprised,
e.g. ouch, wow, bless my soul or a swear word.

CONTENTS

BUYING A NEW CAR

_____ fancied herself as _____

Name of female friend   adjective

when she wore her _____ _____ ,

                              colour   item of clothing

_____ _____ and matching handbag. She

    colour   item of clothing

really looked the business. _____ had

                                 Same name of female friend

decided she would need a brand new _____ to

                                     type of vehicle

match her new status and was visiting the car showroom. She

asked the salesman if he had a _____ model she

                                    adjective

could look at. "I have just the thing for you," he said. "Come

and look at this _____ . It is our latest model

                   type of vehicle

and goes up to _____ miles an hour at _____ miles

               number   number

to the gallon. The metallic _____ shade would

                             colour

really match your _____ eyes. I can just imagine you

                        adjective

driving through _____ sitting behind the

                    Geographical Location

_____ and waving at the _____

  type of vehicle part   plural noun

as you pass by."

BOY MEETS GIRL

This is a page from the diary of _____.
Name of male friend

When I went to a party in _____, I met
Geographical location

_____ for the first time and I was smitten.
Name of female friend

She looked so _____ with her _____
adjective adjective

hair hanging down to her _____. The colour of her
body part

hair matched the deep _____ of her eyes. Her mouth
colour

was _____ and when she smiled she showed her
adjective

_____ _____ teeth. _____ she was
adjective colour Adverb

just the right height for me at _____ feet tall. At _____
number number

stones in weight she had a _____ figure and looked
adjective

a picture. I asked her for a date. _____ I said, "I
Affectionate term

think you are _____ and I would like to take you to
adjective

_____ where we can have a _____
geographical location adjective

time together."

HIGHWAY CODE

1. When arriving at a _____ crossing, you must
                       type of animal

give way to _____ .
            plural noun

2. When reversing around a _____ keep as close to
                      noun

the _____ as possible, look in your _____
      noun   noun

and signal your intentions by waving your _____
                                   body part

out of the window.

3. If a _____ should run into the road in front of your
         noun

car, you must stop _____. Any accidents should be
                 adverb

reported to a _____ as soon as possible.
          type of professional person

4. Take regular rest periods when driving _____
                          adjective

distances. Get out of the _____ , stretch your
                   noun

_____ and breathe in some fresh _____ .
body part (plural)   plural noun

5. It is against the law to drive whilst under the influence

of _____ . Anyone who fails the breathalyser test faces a
   plural noun

_____ _____ and the loss of his _____.
adjective   noun   noun

A DAY OUT AT THE ZOO

It was such a _____ day that _____ and
                adjective   Name of female friend

_____ decided to take a trip to the zoo.
Name of male friend

The couple were eager to feed the _____
                                              adjective

_____ and bought some _____ to give them.
type of animal (plural)   type of food

_____ reached through the bars with his delicacy
Same name of male friend

but _____ the animal mistook his _____ for
           adverb   body part

a _____ and bit off his _____.
     noun   body part

The couple _____ made way to their _____
              adverb   type of vehicle

and set off for the local hospital. The _____ in
                                    type of professional person

the Accident and Emergency department was _____ to
                                        adjective

see the state that _____ had got himself into and
                Same name of male friend

_____ fetched his _____. " _____!"
  adverb   noun   Exclamation

he exclaimed. "We will have to get this _____ fixed
                                   body part

back to his _____ as _____ as we can."
           body part   adverb

The moral of this story is never to feed _____
                                     type of food

to the _____.
   type of animal (plural)

THE BIRTHDAY BOY

Today is a special day; it's the birthday of _____.
Name of male friend

We are going to have a surprise party. We will decorate his

house with _____ _____ and _____
colour plural noun colour

_____. The food will be _____. We will
plural noun adjective

serve _____ sandwiches and _____ flavoured
type of food type of flavour

crisps. For dessert we will have _____ ice cream with
type of flavour

_____ sauce. There will be lots of _____ and
type of flavour type of liquid

_____ to drink.
another type of liquid

We have bought _____ a _____ card with a
Same name of male friend adjective

picture of a _____ on the front. We hope he will like
noun

his _____ present that we bought in _____.
adjective Name of shop

It is a _____ that he can use to play his _____
noun plural noun

on. When he opens it he will say "_____! What a
exclamation

_____ surprise, this _____ is what I've
adjective noun

always wanted."

MY HOBBY

I have a _____ hobby; I collect _____ which I
             adjective   plural noun

keep in a _____ in my _____ . I don't collect
             noun   room of house

the _____ types that are _____ , I prefer the
      adjective   type of shape

_____ types that are _____ . My friend
  adjective   type of shape

_____ thinks I am _____ because he
Name of male friend   adjective

collects _____ which he reckons is more fun.
     plural noun

When I have collected _____ of my _____ I can
           number   plural noun

put them in my _____ . I am going to keep them
          noun

for _____ years after which they should be worth _____
  number   number

_____ . This should be a _____
  plural noun   adjective

investment. I will look up the value of my _____ in
                          plural noun

the _____ catalogue. When they are valuable I will sell
    noun

them to a _____ and _____ I will
    type of professional person   adverb

become a _____ person.
     adjective

Don't you wish you were a _____ collector?
              noun

PROBLEM PAGE

Dear Problem Page,

My name is _____ and for many _____
          Name of male friend   unit of time - plural

I have been in love with a girl called _____ .
                                       Name of female friend

Because I am very _____ I need some advice about
                   adjective

asking _____ out. I think about her all the time
       Same name of female friend

and it's breaking my _____ . She has such _____
                     body part   adjective

_____ eyes, a sensual _____ and _____
 colour   body part   adjective

_____ hair. I can't sleep at night and I would give
 colour

my _____ for a chance to _____ with her.
   noun   verb

_____ is going out with a boy called
Same name of female friend

_____ who is no good. He is _____
Name of another male friend   adjective

and _____ and takes her for granted. Just last week he
    adjective

took her to a party and left her in the _____ while he
                                        room of a house

had a _____ with the _____ . What can I do?
      type of drink   plural noun

Please help me because once this lady gets to _____
                                               verb

with me, I know she will dump that _____ for me.
                                   noun

WEDDING

_____ and _____ were married last
Name of female friend   Name of male friend

_____ by the _____ of _____ .
Day of the week   type of religious leader   Name of a town

_____'s dress was _____ _____
Same name of female friend   colour   type of material

and had a train trimmed with _____ fur.
type of animal

_____ in contrast was more _____
Same name of male friend   adverb

dressed. He wore a long _____ , _____
item of clothing   colour

gloves, _____ _____ and a _____
colour   item of footwear   adjective

_____ . A _____ in his lapel completed his
item of headgear   type of flower

attire. The _____ couldn't believe how _____
same religious leader   adjective

the pair looked and shook his _____ in amazement.
body part

" _____ ! You two look _____ !" he
Exclamation   adjective

exclaimed.

The service went well and the _____ couple left
adjective

_____ in _____ for their honeymoon in
body part   body part

_____ where they had a _____ time.
Geographical location   adjective

AT THE SEASIDE

One day _____ and _____ went to
          Name of female friend   Name of male friend

_____ travelling in a _____ _____
Name of coastal town   colour   type of vehicle

they had hired from _____ . When they got to the
                    Name of shop

beach, the couple decided to make a _____ out of
                                     type of building

sand using a _____ and _____ they had
             noun   noun

bought from the beach café. When it was finished they

put a _____ on the top that blew in the wind.
      noun

Later they hired a couple of _____ to sit on and
                             item of furniture (plural)

have a rest and also a _____ to keep off the sun. They
                       noun

fell asleep for a couple of hours.

When they awoke, the pair decided to look for

_____ in the rock pools. _____
type of marine animal (plural)   Same name of male friend

put his _____ into the water and pulled out a
        body part

_____ . "_____ !" he cried. "Look at this."
noun   Exclamation

He popped the _____ into a _____ full of
              noun   type of container

_____ and they took it home for their dinner.
type of liquid

9

ON THE FARM

Life on the farm is always _____ as there are always
adjective

plenty of jobs to do from morning until _____. The
noun

farmer and all the workers get up early when the _____
type of bird

crows. They milk the _____ and collect the
type of animal (plural)

_____ eggs before breakfast.
type of bird (plural)

On a typical day the farmer has to _____ the fields
verb

and sow the _____. Broken fences and _____
plural noun   plural noun

have to be fixed.

The _____ have to be moved back into the fields
type of animal (plural)

after the milking and the _____ are rounded for
type of animal (plural)

dipping up by the shepherd and his _____ .
type of animal

It is usually well after six o'clock before the work is finished and

everyone comes home for a well earned _____ . Then
noun

it's off to bed where the farmer is asleep almost before his

_____ hits the pillow.
body part

KEEPING A PET

_____ and _____ are the most popular
Type of animal (plural)   type of animal (plural)

choice of pet as they are such _____ company.
                                    adjective

Before acquiring a pet it is _____ to remember that
                                  adjective

you will have to look after your _____ for the rest of
                                        noun

its life. _____ have to be exercised regularly and
          Type of animal (plural)

love to go for a _____ in the park. If you throw them
                      noun

a _____ they will delight in chasing it and bringing it
       noun

back to you to _____ again.
                    verb

_____ are more independent animals but can be
Type of animal (plural)

just as affectionate as _____ . They make
                            plural noun

_____ pets.
   adjective

Smaller pets such as _____ are easier to look after
                         type of animal (plural)

as you can keep them in a cage, or you may want to keep fish.

Fish can be kept in a _____ or _____ of
                          type of container   type of container

_____ . The choice is yours but remember that
   type of liquid

a _____ is a man's _____ friend.
     type of animal   adjective

11

THE GREASY SPOON

_____ is the proprietor of a café called the
Name of male friend

_____ _____ . He cooks _____
adjective   *noun*   *adjective*

food covered in _____ . The décor of the café is
type of liquid

bohemian with _____ tables and chairs, _____
adjective   *adjective*

tablecloths and a _____ floor covered in _____ .
adjective   *plural noun*

Vases of _____ _____ add a touch of class.
adjective   *type of flower (plural)*

Wearing a _____ _____ apron and
adjective   *colour*

_____ _____ , _____ rules the
adjective   *type of headgear*   *Same name of male friend*

kitchen like a _____ .
noun

The speciality of the house is _____ _____
method of cooking *type of animal*

in _____ wine with _____ and
colour   *type of vegetable (plural)*

_____ .
type of vegetable (plural)

We went for a meal there last week and had a _____
body part

ache for a _____ .
period of time

12

MY BEST FRIEND

My name is _____ and my best friend is called

_____ . I am _____ years old and my

friend is _____ . We share our _____ ,

_____ and our _____ with each other as

that's what friends do.

At the weekend we had a game of _____ together.

The object of the game was for me to _____ while

my friend counted to _____ with her eyes shut before

seeking me out. She found me on the _____ in the

_____ . On my birthday we had a party in the local

_____ . My friend bought me a _____ for

my birthday present; it was just what I wanted. We had a disco

and played our favourite music. Our favourite band is

_____ as they make very good _____

music, that we like to _____ to. My friend and I

always have a _____ time together.

13

BAKING A CAKE

Ingredients

200 grams _____

type of food

150 grams _____

another type of food

½ packet _____

another type of food

One cup of _____

another type of food

A pinch of _____

another type of food

Method

Sieve the _____ into a _____ mixing bowl

type of food   adjective

and rub in the _____ . Add all the other ingredients

another type of food

and mix them together using a _____ _____ ,

adjective   noun

until the mixture is a nice _____ consistency.

adjective

Heat the _____ to 180°C. Line a _____

noun   noun

with _____ and grease well. Pour the _____

noun   adjective

mixture into the tin and bake for _____ minutes or

number

until _____ to touch and _____ in colour.

adjective   colour

Turn out onto a _____ and leave to cool.

noun

SAFETY IN THE GARDEN

You would be surprised at how many hazards there are in the

garden. Most of us know that we mustn't leave a rake lying

down with its prongs up. If someone should stand on the end

it may flip up and hit them on the _____ .
                                        body part

_____ _____ should be kept in the tool shed
  Adjective   plural noun

when not in use. When digging you should wear a _____
                                                      adjective

_____ and _____ _____ . Keep
 item of clothing   adjective   item of footwear (plural)

your _____ and steps in _____ condition.
        plural noun   adjective

Check for _____ paving slabs on which people may
              adjective

trip and break their _____ . If you have an electric
                          body part

_____ or hedge trimmer, never try to clear the blades
     noun

when the power is on or you may chop off your _____ .
                                                   body part

To be safe, fit a circuit breaker to the _____ and take
                                              noun

care not to cut through the electric _____ .
                                          noun

Remember you are responsible for your own _____ .
                                               noun

MISTAKEN IDENTITY

_____ is in deep trouble, facing a _____
<small>Name of male friend</small> <small>number</small>

year stretch in _____ prison for
<small>Name of town</small>

_____ smuggling. He was shopped by
<small>type of plant</small>

_____ to protect the real culprit, her lover called
<small>Name of female friend</small>

_____ . _____ is _____
<small>Name of another male friend</small> <small>Same name of male friend – 1</small> <small>number</small>

feet tall, _____ and bald with a _____
<small>adjective</small> <small>colour</small>

beard. _____ is a _____
<small>Same name of male friend - 2</small> <small>adjective</small>

fellow with _____ eyes and long _____
<small>type of animal (plural)</small> <small>colour</small>

hair in a ponytail. He has a limp and uses a _____
<small>noun</small>

to help him walk. Who could mix them up? The local

police suspect _____ is the real criminal and
<small>same name of male friend - 2</small>

want to _____ with him. They believe he should be
<small>verb</small>

captured and locked up in the _____ in the town
<small>noun</small>

square. Local residents would be allowed to throw rotten

_____ at him. Let's hope the police catch him and
<small>type of fruit (plural)</small>

teach him a lesson.

BELLY DANCING

_____ is an Egyptian belly dancer. Every night she

Name of female friend

goes to work in the _____ and dances for _____

type of building   number

hours in front of many _____ men and _____

adjective   adjective

women. She swings her _____ seductively to the

body part

_____ _____ music playing in the

adjective   type of music

background. She wears a _____ made from

item of clothing

_____ material and only her _____ is visible.

adjective   body part

She flutters her _____ and winks _____ at

body part   adverb

the audience, moving her _____ over her body. She

plural noun

has a _____ figure for belly dancing. She is _____

adjective   number

feet tall with a _____ bosom, _____ waist

adjective   adjective

and _____ hips. _____ loves her work

adjective   Same name of female friend

and is paid well at _____ pounds per _____ . She

number   unit of time

really is very _____ and is definitely worth going to

adjective

watch.

POP SINGER

_____ likes to sing _____ music which is
<small>Name of famous singer</small>   <small>type of music</small>

fine, while _____ sings _____ music
          <small>Name of female friend</small>   <small>type of music</small>

which is better. This lady is _____ feet tall, weighs _____
                        <small>number</small>   <small>number</small>

_____ and has a very big _____ which helps
<small>unit of weight plural</small>   <small>body part</small>

project her _____ voice. Awesome! At the
          <small>adjective</small>

_____ one night she sang _____ to a
<small>type of building</small>   <small>famous song</small>

_____ audience and brought tears to their eyes.
<small>adjective</small>

Once she sang a duet accompanied by _____
                              <small>Name of male friend</small>

a _____ eyed, _____ _____ . They
      <small>colour</small>   <small>adjective</small>   <small>nationality</small>

were so _____ they were chosen to represent
      <small>adjective</small>

_____ in the Eurovision song contest.
<small>Name of European country</small>

At the song contest they were voted as number _____ out of
                                          <small>number</small>

all the entrants and they received a _____ for a prize
                              <small>noun</small>

They are now famous stars and are currently on tour in

_____ where they play their _____
<small>Name of European country</small>   <small>adjective</small>

music to the ——————— .
          <small>plural noun</small>

BATHING THE BABIES

Every _____ days _____ bathes her babies in a
number   Name of female friend

_____ _____ in the _____ .
adjective   type of container   room of a house

She has _____ children aged between _____ and _____
number   number   number

years old and it's not easy for her to do this job on her own.

First she fills the _____ with _____
type of container   adjective

_____ . She then takes off the _____
type of liquid   adjective

clothes of her youngest child _____ until he is as
Name of male friend

naked as the _____ he was born. Next she tests the
unit of time

temperature of the _____ using her _____ .
type of liquid   body part

When she is certain that the _____ is not too
noun

_____ she puts _____ in the tub. She
adjective   Same name of male friend

lathers his _____ body with a _____ being
adjective   noun

careful not to get _____ into his _____ .
plural noun   body part

After rinsing him off, she takes him out and dries him with a

_____ _____ . What a _____
adjective   noun   adjective

game.

EGYPT

_____ was a famous ruler in Egypt _____ years
   Name of female friend   number

ago. She was called a _____ and was worshipped as a
                              type of ruler

_____ . She was noted for her _____ body
    noun   adjective

and _____ personality. _____ was her lover
      adjective   Name of male friend

until he was defeated by _____ . _____ ,
                        a famous warrior   Adverb

_____ died when a _____ bit her on the
 Same name of female friend   type of animal

_____ .
  body part

The Egyptians were famous for their _____
                                adjective

achievements in architecture. Using _____ ,
                             plural noun

_____ and _____ , they constructed
  plural noun   plural noun

_____ triangular _____ built out of
  adjective   type of building - plural

_____ . They kept their dead together with all their
 type of material

_____ _____ needed for the afterlife in these
  adjective   plural noun

_____ buildings that are still standing today. The
  adjective

pyramids are one of the _____ wonders of the _____
                  number   adjective

world.

FOOTBALL CRAZY

_____ is a _____ supporter and goes
<small>Name of male friend   Name of football club</small>

to watch his home team play every _____. His friend
<small>period of time</small>

supports _____ and this causes _____
<small>another football club   plural noun</small>

when the two teams play one another.

Today in fact is the day when the teams are playing each other

in the semi-final for the _____ cup. _____
<small>noun   Number</small>

_____ after kick-off _____ passes the
<small>unit of time - plural   famous footballer</small>

_____ to _____ who _____ it
<small>noun   another famous footballer   verb – past tense</small>

off his _____ and into the net. What a goal! The boys
<small>body part</small>

_____ and _____ in excitement while the
<small>verb   verb</small>

crowd roar _____ . Shortly after the goal is scored the
<small>adverb</small>

referee blows his _____ . A penalty is awarded due to
<small>noun</small>

_____ _____ the _____ . The
<small>famous footballer   verb ending in 'ing'   noun</small>

_____ lands in the _____ and an equaliser is
<small>noun   noun</small>

scored. _____ exclaims _____ in delight,
<small>Name of male friend   adverb</small>

"What a _____ match!"
<small>adjective</small>

AGONY AUNT

Dear Aunty _____ ,

Name of female friend

I think my wife has been having a _____ with the

noun

_____ . She goes out gallivanting every _____ .

type of tradesman   period of time

She says she is going to _____ classes, however

subject at school

she goes out wearing her best _____ her most

item of clothing

expensive _____ and her _____ make-up.

noun   adjective

She comes home in the early hours of the morning smelling of

_____ . I don't know what she sees in this guy. He is

plural noun

not as _____ as me. I have _____

adjective   adjective

_____ hair, _____ eyes and a _____

colour   colour   adjective

physique. He is _____ with a _____ head, a

adjective   adjective

_____ belly and _____ feet. I have always

adjective   adjective

been the _____ husband. I _____ hard, do

adjective   verb

lots of _____ around the house and have no

plural noun

_____ habits. What can I do to get her to

adjective

_____ with me again?

verb

BOYS WILL BE BOYS

_____ and _____ are very
Name of male friend   Name of another male friend

_____ children. One day they got very dirty while
adjective

playing _____ in the _____ .
type of game   noun

_____ fell into a _____ _____
Same name of friend -1   adjective   noun

and got his _____ dirty. _____ laughed
item of clothing   Same name of friend -2

so much at the sight that _____ threw a
Same name of friend -1

_____ at him. It was such a _____ shot that it
noun   adjective

hit his friend on the _____ so hard that blood spurted
body part

out and ran all down his _____ . Now they were in
plural noun

trouble, what would their _____ say? She may give
Female relative

them a _____ . The boys decided they would wash
noun

their _____ _____ in a _____ .
adjective   plural noun   type of container

They added some _____ to the _____ water
plural noun   adjective

so that their _____ would come out nice and clean.
plural noun

After _____ minutes the washing was done and the boys had
number

saved the _____ .
noun

23

DOCTOR, DOCTOR

_____ went to see her local doctor as she was

Name of female friend

suffering from _____ . She had some very

type of illness

_____ symptoms. Since she went out on a

adjective

_____ night out with her _____ she had a

adjective　　　　　　　　　　　　　plural noun

blocked _____ a _____ cough and an

body part　　　　　　　adjective

aching _____. The doctor examined her _____

body part　　　　　　　　　　　　　　　　　　body part

with his _____ and took a sample of her _____

noun　　　　　　　　　　　　　　　　　type of liquid

for testing.

"_____ ! " he said. "It looks like you may have caught

Exclamation

_____ disease. I think you have been _____

noun　　　　　　　　　　　　　　　　verb ending in 'ing'

and _____ too much, it's not good for a _____

verb ending in 'ing'　　　　　　　　　　　　　noun

of your age. I want you take _____ teaspoons of this

number

_____ every _____. Your symptoms

type of liquid　　　　period of time

should start to improve after _____ _____ .

number　　unit of time (plural)

I must warn you though to stop _____ or you may

verb ending in 'ing'

_____ before you ought to."

verb

24

STEAM TRAIN

_____ and _____ visited a model
   Name of male friend   Name of female friend

railway and went on a trip on a very _____ steam
                                     adjective

train. They were allowed to sit with the _____ in the
                                 type of professional

engine compartment. The fireman let them put _____
                                        plural noun

on the furnace. This heats up and is used to boil water to

provide _____ power. The steam drives the
             noun

_____ which turns the wheels. The train can go
    plural noun

very _____ and may reach up to _____ miles per
        adjective   number

hour. _____ pulled the whistle, _____
      Same name of male friend   type of sound

it went. The train _____ along through the
                  verb – past tense

countryside passing _____ and _____ as it
                plural noun   plural noun

went. _____ would look up as they passed and would
     Plural noun

_____ at them. Eventually, after they had travelled
    verb

_____ miles the _____ came to a stop at the
 number   noun

_____ and the couple got off. They had a really
    noun

_____ time and came home _____ .
   adjective   adjective

HAIR WASH

_____ works underground in a coal mine. He gets
Name of male friend

very dirty as he digs for _____. He has to have a
plural noun

shower and washes his _____ _____ hair
adjective   *colour*

_____ times a _____. He washes it in a
number   *period of time*

_____ in the _____. He uses a _____
type of container   *room in the house*   *noun*

and some _____ to make a good lather and massages
plural noun

this _____ into his _____ for _____
adverb   *body part*   *number*

_____. He then rinses out the _____ with
period of time   *plural noun*

_____ _____. He puts _____ on
adjective   *type of liquid*   *noun*

his hair after the shampoo as this makes his hair _____
adjective

and _____. After rinsing he rubs his hair dry with a
adjective

nice soft _____ and creates a style using an electric
noun

_____ . He applies gel to keep it _____ , so
noun   *adjective*

that he looks _____ for all the girls.
adjective

Looking in the mirror he exclaims, "_____ ! I look so
exclamation

_____ I'll be the best looking _____ around."
adjective   *noun*

26

PUBLIC HOUSE

In the middle of our village is the local _____ where
type of building

people go to relax, _____ , _____ and be
verb   verb

merry. The pub The _____ _____ is a
colour   type of animal

_____ place full of very _____ people.
adjective   adjective

_____ is one of the regulars and drinks there
Name of male friend

_____ times a _____ . He has been known to drink
number   period of time

_____ pints of _____ in one _____ . This
number   type of liquid   unit of time

makes him drunk and he then makes a fool of himself,

_____ over the tables and _____ with the
verb ending in 'ing'   verb ending in 'ing'

girls. He sometimes falls asleep on the _____ in the
noun

_____ and his friends have to carry him back home to
room in the house

his wife. _____ his wife _____ is used to
adverb   Name of female friend

his ways and sends him to his _____ with a _____
noun   noun

in his ear and without any _____ . The next day
type of meal

_____ would feel very _____ and would
Same name of male friend   adjective

apologise _____ to his _____ .
adverb   type of relative

HUNTING

For many years royalty and _____ people from Britain
                                    adjective

have enjoyed the sport of _____ hunting. Between
                               type of animal

_____ and _____ people ride on _____ over
number   number   type of animal - plural

_____ and through _____ on the chase.
plural noun   plural noun

_____ and _____ decided to join the
Name of friend   Name of another friend

hunters one day. They wore _____ _____
                                    colour   item of clothing - plural

and carried _____ to make their charges go faster.
                plural noun

The hunters took a pack of _____ with them.
                               type of animal - plural

These animals made a lot of noise _____ and
                                       animal noise ending in 'ing'

_____ as they went on the chase.
animal noise ending in 'ing'

After _____ hours the _____ _____
           number   adjective   type of animal

being chased was very _____ and fell to the
                            adjective

_____ exhausted.   The hunters shouted
    noun

"_____ ! We've caught the _____ ."
  Exclamation   noun

Later they celebrated in the local _____ with a few
                                       type of building

_____ of _____ .
type of container – plural   type of liquid

DOG WALKING

I have a _____ and his name is _____.
          type of animal   Name of male friend

Twice a _____ I take him for a long walk. His
          unit of time

favourite walk is in the park. We take the _____
                        adjective

route, past the _____ houses and shops.
            adjective

_____ likes to sniff all the _____ as
Same name of male friend   plural noun

we go past and usually pees up the _____.
                      noun

Because _____ is so _____ people
       Same name of male friend   adjective

often make a fuss of him. They pat his _____
                      body part

and tickle his _____ which he likes very much and
          body part

he wags his _____ in delight. When we arrive at
         body part

the park, I remove the _____ and _____
            noun   noun

from around his _____ so that he can
           body part

run on the _____. I throw him a _____
       noun   noun

or two which he brings back for me to throw again. We really

enjoy our visits to the park, and it's _____ exercise
                  adjective

for my _____.
   type of animal

THE SPACEMAN

_____ has always been very interested in man's

exploration into space and especially the Apollo programme

which was designed to land _____ on the moon

and bring them safely back to _____ .

_____ hopes that one day he will be an astronaut

and fly in a rocket to _____ . He has had this

_____ ambition for _____ _____ so he

must be serious.

Because _____ is very _____ the

Space Agency have invited him for a trial flight in a

_____ that is being launched from NASA's famous

site in _____.

The trip will launch the astronauts into space at _____ miles

and hour and will orbit the _____ _____ times. The

trip should take them _____ _____ .

_____ is so excited, he can't wait.

KITCHEN RULES

1. Always wash your _____ in the _____

body part   type of container

    before handling raw _____ that you are going to

type of vegetable (plural)

    serve to _____.

plural noun

2. Defrost frozen poultry for _____ _____ in the

number   unit of time (plural)

    microwave or overnight in a _____ room before

adjective

    putting in the _____ to cook.

noun

3. It is advisable to wear _____ _____

adjective   item of clothing (plural)

    when taking _____ food out of the oven.

adjective

4. Girls with _____ hair must tie it up with a

adjective

    _____ _____ or cover it up with a with

colour   noun

    a _____ making sure that no loose strands of

type of headgear

    hair are left hanging over the _____.

body part

5. Chefs and kitchen staff should wear _____

adjective

    _____ , _____ _____ and

item of clothing (plural)   adjective   item of clothing (plural)

    striped _____ to protect their clothes.

item of clothing (plural)

SLIMMING CLUB

_____ was putting on weight. She looked at herself
_{Name of female friend}

in the mirror and was horrified to find her _____
_{body part}

and _____ to be _____ _____ bigger
_{body part}   _{number} _{unit of measurement (plural)}

than they were when she was _____ years old. Oh dear!
_{number}

What could she do?

She took her _____'s advice and joined a diet club.
_{relative}

First she to had to stand on the _____ to be weighed.
_{noun}

Then she was given some rules: she could eat as much

_____ and _____ as she liked, but
_{type of food}   _{type of food}

_____ and _____ were banned. Imagine
_{type of food}   _{type of food}

having to survive without _____ ! Then she was told
_{type of food}

she must have _____ meals a day and always sit at the
_{number}

_____ to eat. She must never eat _____
_{noun}   _{plural noun}

between meals and must eat _____ , savouring each
_{adverb}

bite. After _____ _____ on this diet she hopes to
_{number} _{unit of time}

show off her new _____ figure to all the boys.
_{adjective}